CLEVELAND

A CELEBRATION IN COLOR

BY JENNIE JONES

CLEVELAND: A CELEBRATION IN COLOR

INTRODUCTION

WHEN I first moved to Cleveland in 1978, I was immediately struck by the physical beauty of this city and have been inspired to photograph it ever since. This book is an introduction to the city and not a complete guide. It is hoped that CLEVELAND is an inspiration for us all to more fully appreciate the natural and the man-made beauty this handsome city offers.

Cleveland is a magic mix of rivers, a great body of water, heights and low land. The intimacy of our valleys has helped to develop and preserve the rich heritage of ethnic cultures. It is a city which is friendly and welcoming. A "roll 'em up and get things done" city which continues to make major contributions to industry, commerce, the quality of human life and the cultural arts. Cleveland is a city rich in history and is in the full momentum of yet another renaissance. It will enter the 21st century participating with pride.

Cleveland has always been a center of transportation. In the early 19th century, it had access to over 300 miles of canals. In the early 1900's, 5,000 miles of double rail lines and 14,000 miles of single tracks gave it easy access to the East and West Coasts. In the 1940's, most of the Great Lakes fleets were controlled by Clevelanders. Today the city is surrounded by the great Interstate Highway system serving the United States with I71, I77, I80 and I90.

Cleveland was first in lighting, machine tools and public housing. We stand today as one of the major medical, scientific and cultural centers of the United States. In music, theatre, and the visual arts we are "world class", proving our worth again by being named the city to receive the Rock and Roll Hall of Fame.

For the majority of my life I have been intimately involved in the arts as an artist, photographer, art historian and teacher. The camera has now become the center of my creative activities both personally and professionally. I am often seen at strange hours of the day and night, camera in hand, enjoying the many visual images which Cleveland offers. Through the eye of the camera I have explored Cleveland; from the roof tops of most of the major buildings, from open helicopters for a better view, from cherry-pickers to reach the less accessible but very rich details which so many of our buildings offer. Through these excursions I have met wonderful people and have enjoyed many exciting and amusing adventures.

I wish to thank my husband, without whose unfailing support and enthusiasm this book would not have been possible. John Szilagyi, who designed the format and layout, was most generous with his time and invaluable advice. There are many others who have made contributions, but most of all I would like to say thank you, Cleveland, for this outstanding opportunity!

NOTES:

ABOUT THE PHOTOGRAPHS

The majority of the photographs included in this book were taken with an Olympus OM1, 0M2 or OM4 camera body utilizing the following lenses: 28mm, 35mm shift, 50mm and a 75-150mm zoom. The photograph "Night Reflections" was taken with a Mamiya RZ/67 camera and a 50mm lens. Films used included Kodachrome 64, Fujichrome 64 and VRS 100/120.

Designed by John Szilagyi, Inc.
Printed by Gray Graphics, Willoughby, Ohio
Color Separations by Action Nicholson Color, Brookpark, Ohio

TO MY FAMILY

PREFACE

A city's physical character is made up of the thousands of images one observes while approaching the city and moving about through its streets, its open spaces and buildings. It is all the sights and sounds and smells that one remembers about a particular place.

A sameness of architectural cliches, urban graphics, corporate trademarks and street furniture is causing many American cities to look very much alike. The loss of older buildings through deterioration and whole districts as a result of urban renewal programs have eliminated much evidence of regionalism and individuality.

Fortunately, Cleveland still retains a great many physical features that make it a unique city in America. Its location on a river by a lake, the scale of its downtown, its collection of noble buildings and arcades, its sequence of public spaces and parks, its industrial architecture and bridges, its diversity of neighborhoods and the silhouettes of its religious buildings, and its beautiful close-in residential areas all form images that are quite special.

This book lets us see, through the superb photography of Jennie Jones, the beauty in the views we experience every day; in carefully designed buildings as well as in the vernacular. It is a reminder to maintain a continuity of history by preserving the best of the past and to let our future development be guided by our uniqueness.

Peter van Dijk

13

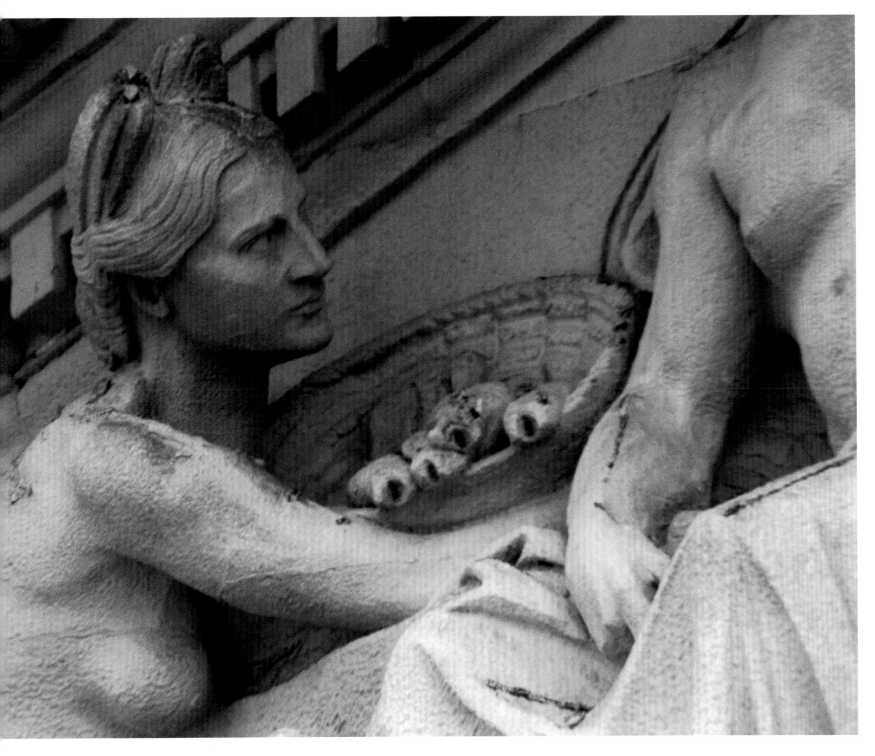

24

29

33

47

54

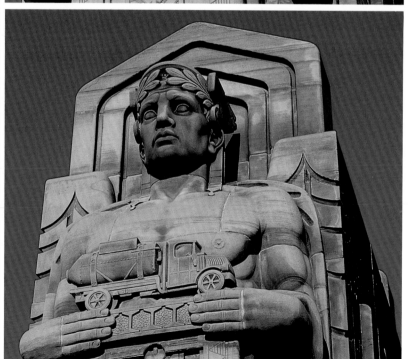

Page 1

SUNRISE IN PUBLIC SQUARE
Tower City Center
Public Square
1930

Soldiers and Sailors
Monument
1894

Page 4

A VIEW REVISITED
Detroit-Superior High
Level Bridge
The Flats
1918
*County Engineer: William A.
Stinchcomb*
*Assistant Engineer: Alfred M.
Felgate*

Page 8

**SUMMER
PERFECTION**
The Flats

Page 2

**FLAGS IN
REFLECTION**
Eaton Corporation:
detail Eaton Center
1111 Superior Avenue
1983
*Arhitects: Skidmore, Owens &
Merrill*

Page 5

PASSING
Ships on the
Cuyahoga River
The Flats

Page 9

BLUE ON BLUE
Main Avenue Bridge
1939
*County Engineer: John O.
McWilliams*
*Consulting Engineer: Wilbur J.
Watson*
Chief Designer: Fred L. Plummer

Page 3

**NIGHT
REFLECTIONS**
Tower City Center
Public Square
1930
Chief Engineer: H.D. Joulett
Contractor: John Gill & Sons
*Architects: Graham, Anderson,
Probst & White*
Medical Arts Building/
Builders Exchange
Building
*Architects: Lundhoff-Bicknell
Company*
Hotel Cleveland
1918

Higbee's
1931

Standard Oil of Ohio
Public Square
1986
*Architects: Hellmuth, Obata &
Kassabaum*

Page 6

**THE BIG SHIPS
COME TO
CLEVELAND**
The Cuyahoga River
from Whiskey Island

Page 10

THE ARCADE
401 Euclid Avenue
1890
*Firm: The Detroit Bridge
Company*
*Architects: George H. Smith and
John Eisenmann*

Page 7

RIVER VIEW
Cuyahoga River and
downtown Cleveland

Page 11

**VENICE IN THE
FLATS**
Higbee Development
Corporation
1973
The Flats

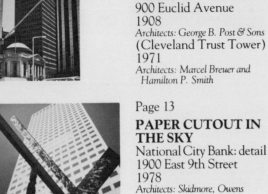

FRIENDS IN THE SKY
Tower City Center
Public Square
1930

Standard Oil of Ohio
Public Square
1986

LIGHT SURFACE
One Cleveland Center:
detail in multiple image
1375 East 9th Street
1981
*Architects: Hugh Stubbins
& Associates*

Page 30

GLOBAL FLIGHT
Cleveland Hopkins
Airport: detail
1976

Sculptor: Clarence Van Duzer

Page 24

**A MAJESTIC
CORNER**
United States Post
Office, Custom House
and Court House: detail
East 3rd at
Superior Avenue
1910
Architect: Arnold W. Brunner
Commerce: detail
1912
Sculptor: Daniel Chester French
Cleveland Public Library
325 Superior
1925
Architects: Walker & Weeks

Page 27

MODERN VIEW
One Cleveland Center:
detail
1375 East 9th Street
1981
*Architects: Hugh Stubbins
& Associates*

Page 31

BEYOND
TRW, Inc.: detail of
sculpture
1600 Richmond Road
1985
Sculptor: Alexander Liberman

Page 28

**CHESTER
COMMONS**
East 12th Street at
Chester
1972

Page 32

**NEIGHBORHOOD
REVIVAL**
Ohio City

Page 25

**REACHING FOR
THE FUTURE**
War Memorial Fountain:
Peace Arising Out Of
The Flames Of War:
detail in multiple
The Mall
1964

Sculptor: Marshall Fredericks

Page 29

PATTERNS
The New Cleveland
Clinic Building: detail
The Cleveland Clinic
Foundation
9500 Euclid Avenue
1985
*Architects: van Dijk, Johnson &
Partners in association with
Caesar Pelli & Associates*

Page 33

WINTER BEAUTY
Ohio City

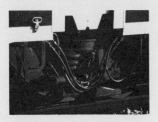

Page 70/Left
Page 70/Right

MYTHICAL MEN
Society National Bank:
detail
Public Square
1889

Architect: John Wellborn Root

Page 74

LION
Ameritrust: detail of the
pediment
900 Euclid Avenue
1908

*Architects: George B. Post
& Sons*

Page 78

WORLD RECORD
September 27, 1986
Aerial

Page 71

**GUARDIANS OF
TRAFFIC**
Hope Memorial Bridge
(Lorain-Carnegie
Bridge): detail
The Flats
1932

*Engineers: Wilbur J. Watson and
Associates
Architect: Frank Walker
Sculptor: Henry Hering*

Page 75

IRON ARABESQUE
Rockefeller Building:
detail
Superior Avenue at West
6th Street
1903-05

*Architects: Wilm Knox and John
H. Elliot*

Page 72

A NEW VIEW
The Hermit Club
1629 Dodge Court
1924

Architect: Frank B. Meade

Page 76

**LIGHT UP
CLEVELAND**
September 18, 1986
Tower City Center from
the Society National
Bank Building

Page 73

AUTUMN
Belgian Village
1928

*Village Plan: Anthony Dinardo
Architect: Harold Fullerton*

Page 77

**LIGHT UP
CLEVELAND**
September 18, 1986
The Mall and the city
from the top of City Hall